D1499612

Inventing Ott

The Legacy of Arthur C. Guyton

Inventing Ott

The Legacy of Arthur C. Guyton

Jerusha Bosarge

QUAIL RIDGE PRESS
Brandon, Mississippi

Library of Congress Cataloging-in-Publication Data

Bosarge, Jerusha, 1974-
    Inventing Ott : the legacy of Arthur C. Guyton / by Jerusha Bosarge.
      p. cm.
    Includes bibliographical references and index.
    ISBN-10: 1-893062-78-3
    ISBN-13: 978-1-893062-78-8
      1. Guyton, Arthur C. 2. Cardiologists--Mississippi—Biography—
    Juvenile literature. 3. Physiologists—Mississippi—Biography—Juvenile
    literature. I. Title.

    RC666.72.G89B67 2005
    616.1'2'0092--dc22   2005018790

First Edition

ISBN-10: 1-893062-78-3 • ISBN-13: 978-1-893062-78-8

On the cover: photos of Arthur C. Guyton;
Guyton's systems analysis of the human circulatory system.
Design by Cynthia Clark
Printed in the United States of America

QUAIL RIDGE PRESS
P. O. Box 123 • Brandon, MS 39043 • 1-800-343-1583
email: info@quailridge.com • www.quailridge.com

Dedicated to

JOEY
for your clever ideas and
unwavering support

JORDAN
for your encouraging smile and
complete confidence in my abilities

and

ABIGAIL
for patiently sharing your mommy
with a computer

Table of Contents

Introducing Ott

The goals of youth are rarely forgotten.
— Arthur C. Guyton

Arthur C. Guyton never thought of himself as extraordinary. Maybe that's what made him so special. He just didn't see things the way others did. It's not that he wasn't insightful. In fact, his perceptiveness was clear by the time he was only three years old, according to his mother Kate. "He could always be depended upon to keep up with the [family's] hats," she once wrote in a letter. Arthur just seemed to be one of those people who took the words of mothers everywhere to heart when they insisted that you can do anything you set your mind to. He set his mind to do many things. After all, one does not become a doctor, a teacher, a scientist, a sailor, a soldier, a radio expert, a writer, an inventor, a husband, a father of ten children (all doctors), and a survivor of paralytic polio without some source of inspiration.

Arthur was born in a small Mississippi town called Oxford on September 8, 1919. It was there, on the quiet, tree-lined streets of Lafayette County that Arthur spent most of his childhood. His home, a white, two-story antebellum, was partially surrounded by a large columned front porch, where the four Guyton children spent many lazy summer afternoons immersed in the Mississippi perfume of oak, pine, and honeysuckle. Just behind the Guyton's house,

Arthur's childhood home in Oxford, Mississippi

Arthur's parents, Kate and Billy Guyton

there was a much smaller house that used to be the kitchen. The reason the old kitchen was in the back yard, is that when the house was first built in 1852, many homes were destroyed by fires that started in kitchens. With the invention of modern appliances, however, the Guytons became quite comfortable living in the same home as their kitchen; thus, the old structure was turned into a home for servants.

The Guytons employed many servants over the years, as Arthur's father, Dr. Billy S. Guyton, was a very busy man. Dr. Guyton, an ophthalmologist (eye doctor), owned a private eye, ear, nose, and throat clinic in Oxford in addition to his teaching position at the University of Mississippi's two-year School of Medicine. Understandably, most of the home and child-care activities fell on the shoulders of Arthur's mother Kate.

Kate Guyton was an extraordinary and lovely lady with soft, dark hair and warm eyes. She had a gentle smile and sunny disposition that made her easy to talk to. Before she married Arthur's father, she was the youngest woman ever sent overseas as a missionary by the Methodist Church. She lived in Soo-Chow, China, for five years teaching mathematics in a Christian school, which is probably the reason Arthur's home in Oxford was decorated with Chinese art. At any rate, when an eighteen-year-old African American girl named Mary Cobb applied for a job helping to care for the four Guyton children, Kate was eager to accept. Mary moved into the Guyton's smaller home, where she lived as a beloved member of the Guyton family for over fifty years.

The Guytons also employed other ladies to help care for the children and around the house. Yet, even under the close supervision of his mother, Mary Cobb, and other caretakers, Arthur's competitive nature still managed to get him into trouble. Once, while on a walk with the maid, four-year-old Arthur was allowed to cross the street alone. What followed would be the first solid evidence of Arthur's insatiable desire to test the boundaries of his abilities. It would not be the last. Just before starting back across the street, Arthur spotted a car. Instead of waiting patiently for the car to pass, Arthur decided to try and beat the car across the street, against the advice of his panicked and screeching caretaker. Unfortunately, the car won the race, and one of Arthur's legs was broken in several places. The pain was terrifying and excruciating for Arthur. Thank goodness chil-

This 1920s Ford Model T is much like the car that ran over Arthur as a young child.

dren are such good healers! Arthur suffered no permanent damage as a result of the accident, except perhaps to his pride.

Arthur became quite a chubby child under the care of Mary Cobb. He loved her cooking. He was so chubby, that he had trouble earning a Boy Scout badge that required him to pass a broad jump test. Mary cooked distinctly southern foods especially well. Her crisp fried catfish and chicken were salted and battered with the skill of a professional chef before being deep-fried to juicy perfection. Mary also specialized in creamy black-eyed peas, collard greens flavored with tender bacon strips, and soft, warm sweet potato pie. Her cooking was a great comfort to Arthur as he healed from his injuries. Arthur so loved to eat as a child, that he could actually put an entire sandwich in his mouth at once. True to his competitive nature, Arthur often used his eating talent to challenge his brothers in fried-oyster-eating competitions. Although he was the youngest of the three, Arthur usually won.

Arthur was the third of four children born to Kate and Billy Guyton. He had two older brothers, Jack Smallwood Guyton and William Franklin Guyton (also known as Bill).

It was Bill who first gave Arthur a nickname that stuck with him well into high school. You see, Bill (just two years old when Arthur was born) could not say "Arthur," and his best attempt at "Art" came out a bit muddled, too. So, just like that, Arthur was "renamed" Ott. According to Ott's son, John, "Until he left Oxford, Daddy was never really called 'Arthur' except perhaps by his mother. Even today, people who grew up with him in Oxford remember him as 'Ott' Guyton, and he bears that name in a book written primarily about William Faulkner." (We will discuss Ott's relationship with the famous Mr. Faulkner more in chapter 3.)

Ott also had a little sister. Ruth Elizabeth Guyton was three and a half years younger than Ott, but she was the

Ott with his three siblings. From left to right: Ott (four), Ruth (five months), Jack (nine), and Bill (seven)

closest to him of all the siblings. Perhaps this was because they were often grouped together as the youngest pair of kids. But oh, how he loved to tease little Ruth. "Ott teased me endlessly," Ruth recalled, "about my big mouth, about my bloomers hanging below my dress, about my crying, about anything." Once, when his mother asked Ott to explain why he teased Ruth so, he simply replied, "I just like to hear her squeal."

But Ott could also be very kind to his little sister. As they grew older, Ott often regarded his sister as his own little project. When he wasn't teasing Ruth, he was teaching her all sorts of things like tennis, bike riding, and swimming. Most of the time, he took very good care of Ruth. Once, while Ott was chasing her through the house, Ruth slammed a door with a glass window in it. The glass fell on Ruth's head, cutting her a little bit, and shattered onto the floor. Now most nine-year-old boys, when faced with such a serious situation, would have cried or asked a grown-up for help. Not Ott. Instead, he bandaged his sister's head, cleaned up the glass, hopped on his bike, and headed for Elliott's Lumber Yard. Ruth recalled Ott's return from the lumber yard. "He was a sight, riding and balancing that two-by-three-foot glass pane on the bicycle handlebars. He repaired the door perfectly before Mama came home, and he admonished me not to tell...but, of course, little sister tattled. I imagine that the same glass is still in that door."

Ott was eight years old when he first learned to ride the bike he took to the lumber yard. He remembered it well, because at that moment, it seemed like the entire world presented itself to him, exclusively for his personal exploration. Every place in town was suddenly within a ten-minute ride, and Ott began to realize that his abilities were only limited by his imagination. He and a bicycle gang of neighborhood boys soon discovered all the steepest hills, the juiciest berry patches, the most bountiful automobile dumps, and the clearest creeks in Oxford. Ott has since proclaimed that his happiest childhood memories were of riding his bike around town. "Ott was very skilled at riding the bicycle," Ruth recalled. "He could even turn around on the seat and ride backwards while it was going," Ott's son, John, explained further. "There is an old home movie of a somewhat older Ott Guyton sitting on the handlebars of a children's bicycle, his feet stretching down to reach the pedals, riding the bicycle backwards around the yard. He did not ride in the street that way, but loved to ride around the big yard, and did it many times."

As his body and spirit roamed freely in the sweet Mississippi breeze, Ott's keen mind soon followed. He grew more curious and creative by the day as he began to discover interests that he never before realized. One of his greatest passions became building. This ambition actually began small. He had always loved making mechanical devices with the erector set given to him by his parents, but he soon began to notice opportunities to solve everyday problems using the engineering skills that he was quickly mastering. One interesting example of Ott's early building adventures began with a desire to go swimming, though he had no swimming pool. The story is described here by Arthur's son, John.

When Ott Guyton was about eleven years old, he and some other boys his age explored the creek that ran through a ravine on the side of Mr. William Faulkner's (his neighbor's) property. They found a spot that was perfect for building a dam of mud and sticks. When the dam was finished and an afternoon thunderstorm filled the creek with water, they were delighted to find that a wonderful swimming hole had been made. They stripped down to their underwear and jumped in the water. It was muddy, but cool all through the hot summer days.

Off to the side was Mr. Faulkner's young stepson, an 8 year old named Malcolm. The boys didn't really try to exclude him, but someone so young really didn't fit in with their fun and their plans. Only on a few occasions would they let Malcolm join in their escapades. Malcolm thought about it and figured out how to get even with the older boys. He pooped in the swimming hole!

When Ott and the others saw what a dastardly deed had been done, they were hopping mad! It wasn't long before they caught Malcolm. They carried him, kicking and screaming, to the swimming hole and threw him in! They thought Malcolm would learn his lesson, and they went home.

Sometime later, Ott was walking toward the Faulkner house. He heard a gunshot! He looked past the old corn field to the crest of a hill in the distance. There was Malcolm with a gun! Of course, Malcolm was not shooting at any person. Just to be safe, however, Ott ran home. It was several weeks before he ventured over to the Faulkner's again.

2

Growing Up
Guyton

*Teachers should allow students to learn,
rather than always simply trying to poke
information into the students.*

—Arthur C. Guyton

As Ott grew older, his building projects became
more complex. Many of his earlier projects were inspired by
Cub Scouting adventures. It was at various Cub Scout
camps that he first got the ideas to build his own canoe and
log cabin. The log cabin project turned out okay, but this is
how Ott described his first attempt at canoe building:

"I enjoyed the canoeing so much that I came home and made a canoe myself, but it was not successful because I did not have the proper equipment to solder the joints (the canoe had been made out of galvanized sheet iron). In retrospect, it was a perfectly good and adequate canoe; the problem was simply that I hadn't had the proper equipment to make the joints, so that the joints did not hold. Any jolt and the canoe would sink. I put it on a lake, and someone else borrowed it, and it probably sank in the middle of the lake, and I could never find it again." Building boats only increased Ott's love of the water. "I only wish that, as a boy, we had had other sports available at that time such as water skiing."

Even without the water skis, Ott spent plenty of time in the water. Over time, he became a competent sailor, and an expert swimmer. His sister Ruth remembers, "As he grew into a youth, Ott became tall and slender, extremely handsome. He became an expert swimmer and diver. To this day, I can picture him on the high diving board, stretching his muscular body into a graceful swan dive, or a twist. All of the girls at the pool were also watching keenly."

But, swimming and sailing were not the only sports that Ott enjoyed. In the wintertime, he excelled at ice skating and skiing, and in the summertime, he played tennis. "We had a tennis court in our backyard," Ruth remembered, "that the boys kept scraped of grass and rolled smooth. Ott had a forceful serve, and long, powerful strokes. He decided that I should have a different serve, to compensate for power. Thus he taught me to put a spin on my serve that

Ott enjoying Sardis Lake on the sailboat he built himself

made it slide along the ground. And he had a friend of his who had been a state champion teach me how to handle a backhand. We spent many afternoons playing together." It was very common for Ott to create logical solutions like these to everyday dilemmas.

A few of the kids you would have seen hanging around the Guyton's tennis court each summer were Mary Elizabeth Glenn (Ott's next door neighbor), Billy Cox (lived a few blocks away), and Billy Mounger. Billy Mounger and Ott became close friends shortly after Billy's father became the minister of the Oxford Methodist Church, where the Guytons regularly attended services. While Mary Elizabeth and Ott were about the same age, the two Billy's were one and two years older. However, Ott and Mary Elizabeth skipped the sixth and tenth grades respectively and caught up with Billy Cox. Although Billy Mounger remained a grade ahead of the remaining three friends, they all attended University High School at the same time.

It was at University High School in Oxford that Ott's abilities became truly boundless. While he was a student there, it seemed like there was absolutely nothing that he couldn't do. In sports, Ott became even more competitive. He played on the tennis team, the track team, and even the football team (only in his final year). Here are Ott's memories of his brief time on the football team at University High School:

"Though it was my first year in football, it was also my last year in high school. I was one year younger than the others in my twelfth grade class because I had skipped a grade along the way. My job was in the middle of the line as guard. It turned out to be an excellent experience." Football, however, was a much rougher sport in the 1930s than it is now, and Ott suffered his fair share of pain as a result. He first learned to play the sport on a rough sandlot near his home in Oxford. On rainy afternoons, the sand would actually grind through his clothes, tearing at his skin during hard tackles. Ott was never intimidated by the pain of his experiences, and in fact recalled these events quite fondly. "My nose was broken twice, once by an opposing player who purposely did it with his fist. I also remember playing in the late fall at night in a post-season game with another conference in freezing weather, and playing with much bigger boys who could flatten me and the others of our team with almost every thrust." Of course, Ott's team lost the game with the bigger boys, but losing did not bother him. It seemed to be the great difficulty of the sport that intrigued Ott the most. He never shied away from a challenge.

Luckily, Ott's high school interests expanded beyond the athletic realm. Although he remained quite popular in high school, he also became much more serious about academics. As the University High School was in many ways a branch of the University of Mississippi (also known as Ole Miss), the school's education was among the most challenging in the state. Strangely though, Ott did not attribute this challenge to the school's curriculum. Instead, Ott is adamant that the academic challenges he faced at University High School originated because of a few teachers who urged him to learn on his own. Perhaps this concept may be better understood explained by Ott himself. Here is how he described his three most influential high school teachers:

One of these was Miss Clyde Lindsey. She was an excellent math teacher who was also willing to teach special courses to those who wanted them. I wanted some extra mathematics that were not normally taught in high school, such as solid geometry, and one other math subject. She gave me a book on this to work massive numbers of problems. Then she would check my work, and so forth. The thing that I learned mainly from this was how to learn mathematics entirely by myself, without any teacher at all other than someone simply to show me how to get started.

Another teacher who influenced me greatly was Mr. Leon Wilbur, who later became Dr. Leon Wilbur.... Part of his PhD thesis work was to teach an experimental class made up of several top students in both the eighth grade, and I believe also the ninth grade. To do this teaching, with students from the two different grades simultaneously, the students were required to perform what was called "contract" work. In other words, the student was responsible for completing all of the activities. It was this responsibility that was exceedingly valuable to me as a student.

The third teacher who influenced me greatly was Dr. R. C. Cook. Mr. Cook was at that time principal of the high school, and didn't have much time available for teaching. He wanted a science program at the school, but he could not obtain adequate science teachers. Therefore he took on the teaching of physics, even though I do not believe that he had much physics in college. He engaged several teaching assistants from the teacher's training program at the University, and they helped him teach the physics course. Because of Mr. Cook's duties as principal, he was not able to even remain in the class more than about half of the time. However, here again, he arranged the material for us to study and the work for us to do, including making available to us appropriate material and laboratory equipment to do special projects on our own.... The willingness of Mr. Cook to help us learn physics, not to teach us physics, taught all of those in that class an extra lesson over and above what one gets in a usual class.

Ott's talent for independent learning naturally spread to his home life. By the time he was in high school, he was the Guyton family's official, self-taught carpenter, appliance

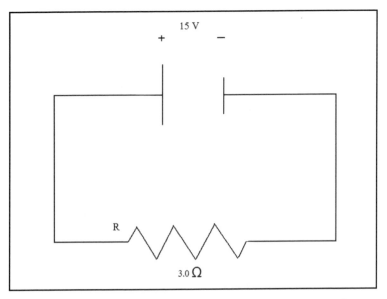

Do you want to learn more about electronics, like Ott? You can begin by studying this illustration of the simplest circuit possible. It has a 15-volt (V) electronic cell, a 3.0 Ohm (Ω) resistor (R), and wires to connect them. Charge flows through the circuit, usually from the positive to the negative end, creating a current of electricity. To find out more about circuits, you may look into any beginning physics book.

repairman, and electrician. There was nothing that he couldn't build, fix, or wire. It was the latter of these skills that would prove most beneficial to Ott's future endeavors. "At the age of thirteen or fourteen, I became seriously interested in electronics, and by the age of fifteen or sixteen, I was building electronic apparatus, including amateur radio receivers, transmitters, and an oscilloscope, a code transmitting system, a code receiving system.... Actually, I had converted one of the rooms in our home into an electronics laboratory. I would read about new electronic circuits, and I would try building them. And then the next day, I would tear those up and build others. It was during one of these summers that I came upon a textbook that gave some of the basics of mathematical analysis of electronic circuits. I studied this in great detail through the summer as well as another 1,000-page electronics physics book, working all of the problems as I went. Therefore, I consider that I have learned electronics more thoroughly than any course that I ever took in high school or in college."

3

Adventures with William Faulkner

It is very difficult for someone to be a truly serious student on a part-time basis.
—Arthur C. Guyton

By the look of things, it would seem as though the older Ott got, the less fun he had. However, nothing could be farther from the truth. The fact is, Ott was one of those people who simply enjoyed learning. It was fun to him. But that was not all that he enjoyed. During his high school years, Ott began to really hone in on his electrical, carpentry, and mechanical skills that he enjoyed so much in his adolescence. "I had interests in building almost anything, building yard furniture; building boats, having built three different boats at one time or another; working around our home — so much so that after I reached high school, I did virtually all of the carpentry around the home, rather than anyone being hired to do this; and I even did small amounts of carpentry around my father's office. Also, as a boy, I saw a person who was an electrician wire a house once, so therefore, I did practically all the wiring that needed to be done around our home. Later, we had difficulty with our oil furnace, and someone had to be called out from Memphis to work on it; however, even these people botched it. I took a large share of what the person from Memphis had done to pieces and reworked it, then put it back together; thereafter it was my job to maintain the oil furnace around the house."

Ott's keen interest in mechanics became more intense as he began to spend time with one of his older neighbors named William Faulkner. You may have heard of Mr. Faulkner, as he has since become quite a famous author! But to Ott he was simply "Mr. Bill." Although twenty years older than Ott, Mr. Bill spent many afternoons playing chess with his young friend on his back porch, or playing croquet with Ott's gang in his very large yard. But the most memorable occasions that Ott spent with Mr. Bill were at the Memphis Airport. "[Mr. Bill] owned one airplane and had an interest in another. One of these was a two-cockpit biplane and the other was a cabin biplane, both made by

Aerial photograph of a Waco UPF-7 biplane

Waco. We would fly around over Memphis all day long in one or the other of the airplanes and, when not flying, we would crawl over all of the other planes. This was a great pleasure and it whetted the appetites of most of us. Several of the kids that he took with him later became pilots, some of them fighting in World War II as pilots, and some making their living for awhile in aviation."

Not all of Ott's flying days were enjoyable, however. Ott's son, John, retells a scary story that his father once confided in him:

> *He drove a car down to the small airport south of Oxford, actually just a vacant cow pasture with a small building, a shed, and a wind sock. Faulkner had invited him to go flying. There was a good breeze that day,*

and they turned the plane into it before gunning the sixty horsepower engine to take off. The airplane rose from the ground. It was tremendously exciting.

But the real excitement came when the engine stopped in mid-air, about half a mile away from the end of the pasture—that is, the runway. Today, novices are taught that if the engine stops after taking off, a pilot should never attempt to turn around and go back to the

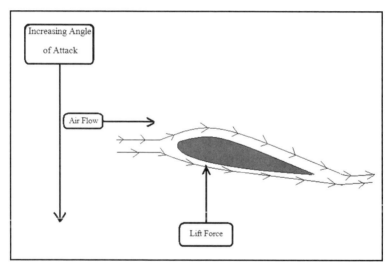

In order for an airplane to LIFT off the ground, we must direct the flow of air over the wings by altering our ANGLE OF ATTACK on the air. The angle of attack is determined by the angle of TILT the wing has in relation to the flow of air. We must tilt the wing of the plane, so that the air that hits the wing will be directed strait down. For every action there is an equal, but opposite reaction (Newton's 3rd Law). So, with the same amount of force the wing exerts on the air in the down direction, the air will return in the up direction (on the wing). This will lift the plane off the ground.

runway. There is not enough lift and momentum to allow the airplane with a dead engine to coast back. Instead, the pilot should look ahead to try to find a pasture or a road where the airplane can land. Back then, however, flying itself was new, and every pilot was a novice.

Faulkner put the airplane into a turn and began to coast back toward the field. It looked as if the wind, still blowing briskly, might save them. The airplane came closer to the field. When they were thirty feet from the ground and falling fast, they had only a few dozen yards to go. Between the airplane and the safety of the pasture were a ditch and a barbed wire fence. At the last instant, Faulkner jerked back on the stick that controlled the ailerons on the tail. The airplane hopped over the barbed wire fence and landed safely. Two of Mississippi's best might have died together that day, but were saved to write their books and go down in history.

About five years later, William Faulkner's older brother Dean took off from the Oxford airport in that same airplane. Nobody knows exactly what happened, but it is speculated that the engine may have stopped. Dean Faulkner died in the crash.

Mr. Bill and Ott also shared two other passions: tennis and sailing. Both friends built tennis courts in their yards, where they spent many afternoons battling for glory. Ott's son, John, describes how the courts were made: "[First] they made posts and strung a net in the middle of the court. [Then] they pushed a large roller to press down the Mississippi red clay dirt on the court [and] used lime to mark the lines. Finally, they set up some tall poles at the ends of the court and strung chicken wire to keep the tennis balls from rolling into the street. Of course, when it rained, they could not play for a couple of days on the homemade dirt court." Ott eventually became such a good tennis player that he made both the high school and college tennis teams. Once, he even qualified as a runner-up in the championship tournament for the entire state of Mississippi!

As he did with most of his teenage interests and hobbies, Ott found a way to pursue his passion for watersports by using his engineering skills to construct his first sailboat. There were two main inspirations for Ott's sailboat construction: First, the United States Corps of Engineers constructed the first sailboat-friendly body of water in Mississippi (Sardis Lake) by damming the Tallahatchie River. Second, his passion was ignited by the passion of William Faulkner (Mr. Bill), who had never personally sailed, but who loved to read about the sport and shared his knowledge with Ott. Here's how Ott described these exchanges:

On many days, as he was passing by, William Faulkner would stop and carry on a long conversation. From books, he had learned all the nautical terms, terms that I didn't know, and terms describing different parts of the sailboat. He would talk about the 'rabbet'

William Faulkner sailing Ott's boat on Sardis Lake

here and the 'keel' here and the 'transom' there, and so forth. Then he would talk about sailing to starboard, sailing to leeward, and other phrases like that. These terms I didn't know, though I was the one who was building the boat.

When I completed the boat, I invited Mr. Bill to sail with me on occasion, and again, we all reveled in his discussion of the art of sailing. I don't think he had actually sailed ever before, but he knew all about it from the books he had read or studied. He enjoyed those outings on Sardis Lake. Later, when I developed polio and thought that I would never use a sailboat again, I sold my boat to him for $300, which would be the equivalent of $1,500–$2,000 today. Actually, I suspect that the boat was worth quite a bit more than that, because it was a well-made boat that we enjoyed immensely.

4

Becoming a Man

The basic theory of calculus
changed my whole way of thinking...
it was a course in logic.

—Arthur C. Guyton

While Ott was in his junior year of high school, his father (Dr. Billy Guyton) became dean of the University of Mississippi's two-year medical program in Oxford. As you may remember from chapter 1, Ott's father was also an ophthalmologist with a private eye, ear, nose, and throat practice called the Guyton Clinic. Dr. Guyton continued to run the Guyton Clinic, despite the increased demands of his new job as dean. Because of this, Ott began to spend a lot of time in the Guyton Clinic to be nearer to his busy father. In true Ott style, he immersed himself in the intricacies of all things medical. Ott was even allowed to observe a few surgical procedures at the local hospital performed by one of his father's friends, Dr. J. C. Cullen. Before he even graduated from high school, Ott had a job in his father's clinic refracting eyeglasses. It was Ott's work refracting eyeglasses that ignited his interest in physics.

You may be wondering what physics has to do with refracting eyeglasses, or even what refraction means. Actually, the two have a good many things in common. In order to fully appreciate the connection, however, there are a few definitions that you may want to glimpse. After scanning the definitions, and reading a general explanation of basic eye-ball mechanics, the idea that follows will explain how Ott became interested in physics from constructing eyeglasses.

matter - (*Oxford American Dictionary*): A physical substance that has mass and occupies space (In other words): ***A thing***

energy - (*Oxford American Dictionary*): The ability of matter or radiation to do work (In other words): ***The amount of strength "a thing" has to work with***

physics - (*Oxford American Dictionary*): The study of the properties and interactions of matter and energy (In other words): ***The study of the way things work***

Now you may be interested to know that the human eye is not just a round ball stuck inside a round socket. Rather, it is one of the most complex and mysterious organs of the human body. Some fundamentals of optometric study include the basic knowledge of the eye's anatomy, light refraction (bending the angle of light), and electro-chemical interaction. For example, unless you are using Braille right now, you are able to read the words on this page because a particular arrangement of light is entering your cornea, making a sharp turn at your lens (refracting), before coming to a halt at your optic nerve. There, the light is actually undergoing a chemical reaction (it changes form) and becomes a sort of electrical energy. The nerve acts as an electrical wire sending the light's electrical message to your brain, which then sees this information in "black and white" so to speak. Pretty complicated, right?

The general idea is this: Since physics is the study of the way things work, and the way the eye works is so complicated, it is easy to understand how Ott was intrigued by physics after working in his father's eye clinic refracting eyeglasses. The fact that the physics of the eye is so challenging was probably the reason the subject held his attention for so long. Ott fell in love with physics.

By Ott's senior year of high school, it was time to choose a career path. This was a particularly difficult time for Ott, because it meant that he would have to limit his courses of study. As you probably realize, Ott was not used to limits. In the beginning of his senior year, he had narrowed his

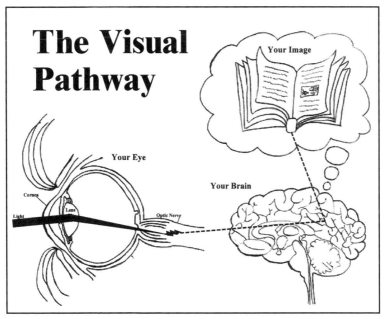

The Visual Pathway

Your Image

Your Eye

Your Brain

Cornea

Light

Lens

Optic Nerve

Light enters the cornea, refracts (bends) through the lens, then transforms into electrical energy at the optic nerve. This nerve acts as a wire, transmitting the light message to the brain, which translates the message into a recognizable image.

choices down to three of his favorite subjects: engineering (because he loved building and inventing), physics (because he loved trying to figure out how things work), and medicine (because he was naturally good at it, interested in it, and it offered job security). By the middle of the year, his choices had narrowed to physics and medicine. In the end, it was the national economy that dictated Ott's decision.

In the 1930s, America was experiencing a money slump called the Great Depression (a time period where almost everyone was poor, and there were not enough jobs available). Although, by Ott's senior year, the worst part of the Great Depression was over, it left most American citizens with a sense of insecurity. The mood of the American population at the time was one of careful skepticism. Ott was no exception, and there were simply not as many jobs in physics as there were in medicine. To Dr. Billy Guyton's relief, Ott decided to follow in his father's (and his older brother Jack's) footsteps, choosing medical school rather than a career in physics. "I have always been happy that I took that choice," Ott reflected. "It did work out beautifully to meld together my background in physics and other physical sciences with my future in medicine."

Once Ott had made the decision to study medicine, his senior year became much less stressful. Ott used this brief lull in educational activity to fully commit himself to having some fun! One of the more memorable experiences of Ott's senior year was a hobo party. All of the students, including Ott, adorned themselves in their finest filthy rags to attend. Another party that Ott attended that year was at Rowan Oak, which is what "Mr. Bill" Faulkner's huge house was named. It was a garden party hosted by Cho-Cho Franklin, Mr. Bill's stepdaughter. Other senior gatherings Ott enjoyed included picnics, a formal dance, parties at Spring Lake, and a scavenger hunt. But, the wildest times Ott and his friends enjoyed that year were the "storms." Ott's friend, Itsie Glenn Cox, described them best. "We used to do a lot of "storm parties," which I certainly wouldn't recommend at all, as I don't know how we managed to get away with them. A group of us would get together and we would say, 'Why don't we go to somebody's house tonight and surprise them with a party?' and we would do that. When the door opened, we'd all be standing there."

Despite all the partying, Ott graduated from University High School on May 29, 1936. He was only sixteen years old and valedictorian of his class of seventy-one students. By the following fall, Ott had begun college at Ole Miss (also known as the University of Mississippi), where his father was dean of the two-year medical program. He planned to graduate, go to medical school, then get a job in academic medicine, so he could teach and research all things medical.

Ott loved his years at Ole Miss. Mostly he loved the methods his professors used to teach the students, or should I say the methods they used to help the students learn. "For the most part, I learned by myself, but with proper leadership from the teachers. I really wouldn't want a different type of training, and I suspect that I got a much better background in physical sciences at Ole Miss than I ever could have gotten at one of the major universities such as Harvard, Yale, or Princeton."

Perhaps one of the most important things he learned at Ole Miss was to combine sciences. He used principals of physics to understand biology, principals of calculus to understand physics, principles of chemistry to understand anatomy, and so on. His study of physics in particular became much more serious. "In physical sciences, every detail of a mathematical equation is absolutely essential, not just desirable—absolutely essential." Ott also learned to love calculus at Ole Miss. "When one goes back to the basics, he can solve almost any problem in calculus, even though no formula may be available."

Just as he did in high school, Ott excelled academically and socially at Ole Miss. He joined a fraternity, Sigma Alpha Epsilon, and the tennis team right away. Before long he was a member of many diverse clubs and organizations including the debating team, Scribblers (a writing group), and the Pre-Medical Club. While attending Ole Miss, Ott also won many honors: Phi Eta Sigma (a national honorary scholastic fraternity), the honor role, first prize in a short-story contest (which paid for a trip to the Southern Literary Festival), the Taylor Medal for superb work in physics (Ole Miss's highest academic honor), and many others.

Although Ott's usual pattern of social and academic excellence remained intact throughout his three years at Ole Miss, something major changed. By the time he graduated in 1939, a full year sooner than his peers, he no longer wanted a career in academic medicine. Instead, Ott set his sights on one of the most difficult and prestigious medical schools in the world to learn surgery. He graduated at the top of his class, packed his bags, and moved to Boston, Massachusetts. Ott was going to Harvard.

5

Medical School and Marriage

Almost every day of my life at Ole Miss had been a great pleasure. It was a time of memory that would make one always want to return to Mississippi.

—Arthur C. Guyton

It was not long after leaving his friendly and beloved Mississippi that Ott started to think he had made a big mistake. His initial impression of the students at Harvard Medical School was that they were generally cold, calculating, or unusually reserved. Students would often hide research materials, sabotage the assignments of others, or commit other underhanded deeds to secure a high ranking in their class. Many of the students were so competitive academically that the administration had to stop telling them their grades, so they wouldn't know who to compete against. As if the cut-throat atmosphere wasn't bad enough, Ott also had to deal with an entirely new method of learning, which he despised. "During my first half year at Harvard, I literally hated it. I was not able to use any of my physical sciences. I was studying anatomy, and rather low levels of chemical memorizing related to some of the chemicals in the body, and some of the biological aspects of the human being, without much understanding of the detailed means of function of the human being. Therefore, I thought that I had made a terrible mistake in going into medicine. What I had not realized was

Arthur, third from the left, with fellow Harvard interns, 1942

that I had entered a field that was entirely new to me, and the first part of the training has to be an introduction to the language of the new field. That is exactly what I was getting...."

As time passed, Ott began to find some value in his Harvard education. As his courses advanced, he began to understand the connection between what he was being forced to memorize, and the big picture of the human body. This understanding was enhanced during his courses of biochemistry and physiology.

Ott absolutely loved physiology, and he even inquired about doing some extra work on the side in this subject with Dr. Walter Cannon, head of the physiology department. However, Dr. Cannon developed cancer and was unable to direct his study. Ott's request was denied.

Luckily, the head of the biochemistry department, Dr. Baird Hastings, took notice of Ott's talent. Ott liked biochemistry, especially the physical aspects of it. He had actually developed his own theory for figuring out how many and what types of ions (or charged particles) are in a solution. Dr. Hastings was so excited about Ott's theory that he assigned Ott his own laboratory to develop his theories using the school's equipment. Dr. Hastings' initial intentions were to directly supervise Ott's lab work, but with the arrival of World War II, Ott's mentor's attention was redirected towards the war effort. This left Ott free to learn and experiment completely on his own, using virtually any methods he desired to learn any subject he wanted! When left to his own devices, Ott's curiosity and ingenuity led him back to his roots in electronics. Using this broad base of knowledge, Ott delved deeply into the mysterious world of electro-chemistry.

During this period of creative and scientific exploration, Ott never abandoned his first love of building. Eventually he realized that from a machinist's perspective, there was no better place to be than Harvard University. Here is how Ott explained it: "In the Department of Biochemistry, there was a small machine shop. I had never in my life been exposed to a metal turning lathe or other metal-working machine tools. Now I had them at my fingertips and could use them in the evenings. I began to work out various types of recording apparatuses for use in patients, and tried to build these in the machine shop. Here again, I did not have enough time and was not very successful in getting finished products. But the experience proved to be invaluable later in life when I did go into research on a full-time basis."

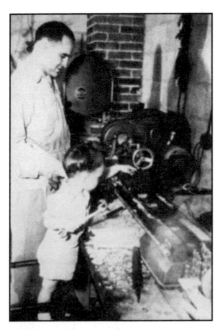

Ott is teaching son Steven (age four) how to use a metal lathe.

One of the devices Ott tried to build during his time at Harvard was an electronic pressure measuring apparatus. Although he never finished building this device at Harvard, he did manage to produce one much later, while serving in the military. He eventually showed his prototype to an instrument manufacturer in Boston, who later developed the first commercial electronic sensing apparatus for measuring arterial pressure based on Ott's design. Doctors still use these today by inserting a tiny transducer into the human body through a catheter in the patient's vein. By using these for the most critically ill patients, doctors have an immediate and constant value that can be used to determine many life-altering processes; for example, how much blood is getting to the heart, whether the patient needs more fluids, and how to adjust their care accordingly. It is a much more accurate method of measuring blood pressure than the crude blood pressure cuffs that you and I have seen in doctors' offices. Ott never received a dime of payment for his contributions to this invention. He never wanted any.

Another device Ott developed at Harvard was an instrument used to provide intermittent suction through tubes inserted into the gastrointestinal tract during surgery. This device removed gases and liquids from obstructed bowels much more efficiently than the old continuous suction apparatus. This invention later attracted enough attention from the right people to alter the course of Ott's future military career. (You'll learn more about this in chapter 6.)

Ott graduated from Harvard Medical School in 1943, with one of the highest academic averages in his class. As usual, he completed his training simultaneously with several extracurricular activities. He maintained memberships in various societies like Alpha Omega Alpha (an honorary medical scholarship fraternity), and the Boylston Medical Society. He was also the official prosector for the dissection and demonstration of cadavers for the instruction of other students. (In other words, he carefully sliced up dead human bodies so that other medical students could see all of the parts clearly.) All of this he did while keeping up his grades and completing a student research fellowship in biochemistry. But these are not the things that Ott valued most about his time at Harvard Medical School.

When he first met Ruth Weigle, Ott had no idea that she was the girl of his dreams. It was a cool, sunny afternoon during his first year at Harvard when Ott had some rare time away from his studies. He and a friend decided to take a bike ride. And what better place for a tall, lean, good-looking young college man to visit than a women's college? There happened to be a private women's institution for the study of liberal arts about fifteen miles west of Harvard. As Ott was never the "all-work-and-no-play type," he and his friend decided to visit Wellesley College. While riding around campus, the boys saw someone they recognized from a party they had all once attended. The young lady had with her a slim and beautiful, bright-eyed brunette named Ruth Weigle. As the conversation dwindled, the foursome parted ways without the slightest inkling that someday soon, half of them would be joined in matrimony.

Not long after their initial introduction, Ott actually became quite serious about another Wellesley College girl. Oddly, this young lady happened to be one of Ruth Weigle's very best friends. As time passed, Ott and Ruth's friend even discussed marriage. But as they got to know each other's families, it became apparent to both of them that they were not as perfectly matched as they initially thought.

By the time Ruth found out about their break-up, Ott was already dating another girl. Being a handsome, intelligent, ambitious, and athletic young man with a captivating southern charm, Ott was quite a catch. Realizing this, Ruth decided to take a rather aggressive approach to dating than one might have been accustomed to in the 1940s. She asked Ott for a date. Luckily, Ruth's direct approach paid off, and before they knew it, the couple were chaperoning a formal dance at Pine Manor Junior College, where Ruth had recently been hired as a teacher. Ott recalled:

> *We were hardly chaperones, because we were enjoying the party as much as the girls for whom the party was being given. At any rate, things moved extremely rapidly, because Ruth and I had very, very many things in common—much more than I had had with her friend. For instance, Ruth's father was a professor at Yale University and he was also dean of the Yale Divinity School, while my father was professor*

at the University of Mississippi and was dean of the University of Mississippi Medical School. Therefore, we both had an academic background. Also, Ruth had been at the very top of her class at Wellesley, and I had usually remained either at the top or close to the top of my classes through school, so that we were both devoted to educational pursuits. And another thing that I liked tremendously about Ruth was her vivacity, her interest in almost everything, and even the fact that she went with me to a wrestling match—but that was before we were married, never after we were married. So I did learn that part of that interest was in me, and not wrestling.

Ruth's college degree was a Bachelor of Arts in Biblical History. Her initial plans were to continue her education in pursuit of a Ph.D., but plans changed when one month after the Pine Manor dance, Ruth and Ott were engaged to be married. On June 12, 1943, the couple was married on the Yale University campus in New Haven, Connecticut. Ott's younger sister, who was also about to be married, recalled her version of Ott's wedding. "At the close of the wedding ceremony, Ott, in his thorough way, gave Ruthie a long, long kiss. Later, Mama confided in me, 'Billy (my father) was terribly embarrassed. Ruth, when you and Keith are being married, you must not let him kiss you in the ceremony; it would just kill your father. It just isn't done in the South.' We didn't."

Ott married Ruth Weigle June 12, 1943, in New Haven, Connecticut.

6

A Change of Plans

*I would advise anyone setting up a
training program in any clinical field
not to overwork the students...without
giving them probably at least half of their
time to dip deeply into what other people
have learned through their writings that
are published in the library."*

—Arthur C. Guyton

On January 1, 1943, just months before his marriage to
Ruth, Ott began his surgical internship at Massachusetts
General Hospital. The break-neck pace of the program was
grueling. "My first year of internship, which was in surgery,

had times of real delight and other times of not much fun. The times when it wasn't much fun, it was because we were overworked and too tired. It was not much fun to me at times when I would stay up all night long and then have to go to the operating room the next day. Fortunately, the work in the operating room was so exhilarating because I had always loved to use my hands, that the lack of sleep throughout the night made little difference. But when the operating schedule was over, and we were beginning to see patients and work up new patients for operations the next day, then would be the time that the fatigue would set in and one wondered whether or not it was all worthwhile."

Before Ott could finish his internship at Massachusetts General Hospital, Uncle Sam called him into military service. You see, Ott had been a member of the Naval Reserve for several years, and the country was at war. Ott did not shirk his duty to his country. On January 1, 1944, he began his active duty in the United States Navy, having been commissioned lieutenant, junior grade. Ott was very proud to be a sailor and to serve his country.

Unlike many of the boys he knew, Ott was

Lieutenant Junior Grade Arthur C. Guyton, U.S. Navy

This is how the Naval Medical Center in Bethesda, Maryland, looks today.

not assigned to missions overseas. Thanks to a previous invention (the intermittent suction device from chapter 5), Ott's fate was in Bethesda, Maryland. The device he invented impressed a man named Dr. Henry Allen, who happened to be the head of one of the principal surgical services at Massachusetts General. So much did it impress him, that upon learning of Ott's military commission, he wrote a letter to the head of the Department of Surgery at Bethesda Naval Hospital requesting a military/surgical position for him there. Thanks to Dr. Allen's letter, Ott was placed in charge of Bethesda Naval Hospital's "tube service program" for the first few months of his military career. "This turned out to be a boon, because I was not overworked in performing surgery…. This gave me the opportunity to have almost total freedom every afternoon, despite the fact that a war was on. Furthermore, the Surgeon General's library was at this hospital. With a beautiful library, and with the time on my hands to study, my time in the Navy was one of the most delightful periods of our lives." Ott learned everything there was to know about surgery: techniques, procedures, equipment, theories, and research.

Ruth was not with Ott during his first few months in Bethesda, as she was expecting the couple's first child. During this delicate time, she decided to stay home with her parents for additional support. Baby David Lee Guyton was born on April 16, 1944, in New Haven, Connecticut. When baby David was about a month old, Ruth finally felt well enough to travel. She and chubby little David joined Ott in Bethesda, where they soon rented their first home together (or, more specifically, the first floor of a home) about fifty miles outside of town in

Ott and Ruth with their first child, David Lee, April 1944

Braddock Heights, Maryland. Their new home was very close to Camp Detrick, the location of Ott's next assignment.

Not long after Ruth's arrival, in the spring of 1944, Ott was transferred to the Bacterial Warfare Department in Camp Detrick, Maryland. Here Ott spent the remainder of his military service doing research in bacterial warfare that ultimately led to one of the greatest honors he ever received, an Army Commendation Citation. Since his military discoveries were so important and beneficial to our country, they are best described in Ott's own words:

On arriving at Camp Detrick, I did not know whether I could ever fit in. However, I was given several weeks to study, and to study all the different types of research programs and the different types of bacteria

This is the World War II Research Center at Camp Detrick, Maryland. 1941

that were being contemplated for use, the different types of toxins from bacteria that might be used, and so forth. Using that time, I put together a survey of all those aspects of bacteriological warfare where my own background training might fit. There were two aspects where it did fit quite well. One of these was in devising physical types of apparatus, especially electronic apparatus, to detect aerosol clouds. An aerosol cloud is a cloud of small particles. In this case, we were interested in clouds of small particles of bacteria or viruses or toxins. Therefore, I spent a good share of my time

Camp Detrick, Maryland, in the 1940s. Research personnel worked in buildings designed for safety, protecting them, the community, and the organism from contamination. Air was filtered, drawn by negative pressure from room and cabinet systems.

Camp Detrick, Maryland, in the 1940s. Researchers worked in one of several size aerobiology chambers developed at Camp Detrick for work on microbial aerosols and the spread of disease.

during the next two years devising different types of devices to detect particles in the air. One of these turned out to be reasonably successful…[as it was able to] give one an idea of the size of the particles in the air and how many particles there were.

In addition, other people began to get me to work on electronic apparatus for other uses around the research compound…. Therefore, I worked on other types of electronic apparatus, such as photo flash control apparatus, or studying the dispersion of particles from exploding bombs by photographic means, and so forth.

Another project that fit with my background was to develop the appropriate electronic recording equipment for studying the action of the toxin called botulism... which is one type of food poisoning. The botulinus bacterium releases this toxin into spoiled food and it can cause paralysis of the person who eats the food. The idea of using the botulinum toxin in warfare came from the fact that purified botulinum toxin is so lethal, that one gram of it, if dispersed equally among four million people, could paralyze all of these people and kill them. One of my jobs... was to determine how the toxin acted on the human body and other aspects of its physiological effects.

After two years of research at Camp Detrick, the war ended. A few months later, Ott was honorably discharged from the military. The year was 1946, a year that would turn out to be one of the most defining periods of his life.

7

Tragedy Strikes

I did learn to use the muscles I still had,
and I've gotten along fairly well now
for over forty years on crutches and using
a wheelchair during most of the day.

— Arthur C. Guyton

Before returning to Boston to resume his surgical internship, Ott took a job teaching physics for one year at Hood College, a girl's college in Frederick, Maryland, located about six miles from Camp Detrick. The college was desperately short of professors, and the Navy was able to keep him listed as active duty until the spring, so Ott was happy to help. Little did he know, he was enjoying some of the last truly care-free days he would ever have.

After Ott returned to Boston, his career finally seemed to be coming together. He had decided to specialize in cardiac surgery, despite an opportunity to become chief resident of the neurology department at Massachusetts General. Also Dr. Edward Churchill, the head of the surgery department, gave him a research lab to use for his own experimentation. For Ott, life couldn't have been better.

But life was not as pleasant for Ruth and baby David. Due to a shortage of housing following the return of World War II soldiers, the Guytons were forced to live in a tiny, crowded apartment complex while their new house was being built. Since Ott's busy schedule kept him away from his family most of the time anyway, Ruth decided to move into her parent's home with David until their house was ready.

In late September of 1946, the Guytons moved into their new home in Wellesley, Massachusetts, the same town in which Ott and Ruth first met. Together, they made their house into a home, complete with a workshop in the basement where Ott built most of their furniture. In addition to working on household projects, he also planned to use his basement workshop to build equipment for his research in the lab at Massachusetts General. But plans changed.

By mid October, Ott's work schedule was unbearable. At one point, he had been working for 120 hours (more than four days and nights) without sleep. He tried to sleep some during this time, but a severe pain in his lower back made rest impossible. During the last two days of this long working period, Ott spiked a very high fever and felt exhausted, but his pride would not allow him to leave work. "I was too ashamed to leave my patients, putting extra loads on the other residents who were equally as tired as I," Ott explained. But he was wrong. The other residents were not equally as tired.

Ott finally visited the emergency ward when he could no longer urinate. His bladder was so full that he felt excruciating pain, as though something was stabbing into his belly. He was desperate for relief. Ott was only slightly surprised when the hospital placed him in isolation. By this time, the seriousness of his medical situation was beginning to sink in. Here is how Ott described his diagnosis:

> *The first diagnosis that was made by the neurologist who saw me and who studied the back pain and other symptoms, was I probably had tuberculous meningitis. At that time, no one, I believe, had ever lived through a bout of tuberculous meningitis.... It turned out that I was very fortunate that I did not have [that disease].... During the night, I reached over for something on the table next to my bed and found that my left arm, with which I was reaching, would not rise. When this happened, I made the diagnosis myself, for I knew that I had polio.*

Ruth's reaction was total shock. At the time, she was pregnant with the couple's second child. When she was notified that Ott was ill, she was simply told that he had ignored a high fever and was now in a hospital bed. When Ott told her that he had paralytic polio, she couldn't believe her ears. "At first, I couldn't accept it. My husband was six feet tall, a powerful man with muscular legs. He went up stairs two at a time. Now I was told he might never walk again."

Paralytic polio is a virus that a person can catch just like any germ, especially when his or her immune system is low. It infects the human body, and then spreads to the spinal cord, damaging it often to the point of severe paralysis. Today, most Americans are immunized against this disease by getting a series of shots (containing vaccines) when they are very

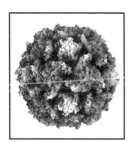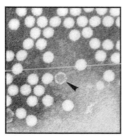

Left: Illustration of the polio virus
Middle: Transmission electron micrograph of poliovirus type 1
Right: Scanning electron photomicrograph of polio virions

The poliovirus lives in the human pharynx and intestinal tract. Poliomyelitis is an acute infection that involves the gastrointestinal tract, and occasionally, the central nervous system.

young. However, at the time of Ott's infection, this shot (or inoculation) had not yet been invented. From that night in the hospital, when his hand failed to obey his brain's command, until the day he died, much of Ott's body was paralyzed.

Ott soon realized that finishing his surgical residency would be physically impossible. He had permanently lost feeling in (and use of) his left-upper arm, both of his shoulders, and his right lower leg. One month after Ott's grim diagnosis, Ruth delivered their second baby, Robert Allan Guyton. He was born November 23, 1946, but because of his paralysis, Ott was not able to hold him.

Two months later, the Guytons moved to Warm Springs, Georgia, where Ott spent the next seven months recuperating and strengthening the few muscles in his body that he was able to regain the use of. Warm Springs is a little town just south of Atlanta containing all of the richness and beauty that nature could cram into 4,200 acres. The fragrant forest, crystal clear streams, and lush green mountains all contributed to the healing powers of the town's famous warm springs. The fresh warm breezes of the South, perfumed with oak, pine, and sweet magnolia, reminded Ott of his beloved Mississippi, warming his heart as he was carried from the train.

The springs begin at a source in the mountains, and somehow remain a constant 88°F all year long. It was the warm waters of Warm Springs that attracted the attention of polio survivors around the world. Among these polio survivors was a former president of the United States named

Franklin Delano Roosevelt. In fact, it is because of the benefit that President Roosevelt received from the warm springs that he created the Georgia Warm Springs Foundation in 1927, where Ott now resided. Incidentally, President Roosevelt's home in Warm Springs became widely known during his presidency as "The Little White House," because of how much time he spent there.

Indeed the year 1946 seemed like a very bleak one for Ott. Yet while most people would have been pretty depressed, or even bitter about the way that things were turning out, self-pity was never Ott's style. His determination was only strengthened by his hardship. "It was clear that I couldn't be a surgeon as I had planned. But that meant I could devote myself to the two things that meant most to me: medical research and raising a family." Ott wasted no time getting started.

Ott, Ruth, and David enjoying a picnic in Warm Springs, Georgia, 1946

While still in Warm Springs, Ott began to put his disability to work as a creative inspiration. He studied the patients there and compared their complaints and ailments to his own disability. From his observations, Ott began to invent machines that could improve the lives of his fellow polio sufferers. He began by creating a "walking" leg brace that was much more comfortable and easy to use than the other medical walking devices available at the time. Another of Ott's inventions was a type of hoist for humans, so they might be lifted from one place to another with greater ease to the lifter and greater comfort to the lifted. He also invented a new type of electric wheelchair that could be controlled by the use of a "joystick," which is still the most widely used version of the wheelchair in use today. Ott's compen-

In 1947, Ott demonstrated the first electric wheelchair to a panel of doctors just before receiving the Presidential Citation for his invention.

sation for these life-improving inventions was negligible, and he rarely even used them himself. When asked his reasons for inventing them in the first place, Ott simply responded, "I just wanted to see if I could do it." He simply refused to make money off of the suffering of others. Ott later received a Presidential Citation for his invention of the modern electric wheelchair.

8

From Tragedy to Triumph

*One begins to learn that awards and
prizes are partially due to being prepared,
but to make that truly astounding
discovery requires a tremendous
amount of luck.*

—Arthur C. Guyton

Ott and his fellow doctors and therapists eventually had to admit that he had received all of the physical benefits that Warm Springs had to offer him. It was time to go home. But, where was home? Though Ott had several job offers in

Boston, that was never truly his home. Having healed his body to the best of his ability, it was time to heal his soul. In the fall of 1947, the Guytons moved back to the small town of Oxford, Mississippi. Ott was finally home.

Ott, Ruth, David, and baby Robert first moved into a home owned by Ott's father. Dr. Billy Guyton (now known as "Pop" to his grandchildren) no longer served as dean of the University of Mississippi School of Medicine, but Ott was still able to secure a job teaching there in the Department of Pharmacology. At the same time, Ott began teaching physiology three times per week in Memphis at the University of Tennessee Medical School. It didn't take long to realize that he was enjoying his three days a week in Memphis more than his full-time position in the pharmacology department. Physiology was his true passion.

Understandably, when Ott was offered a full-time position at the University of Tennessee Medical School Physiology Department, he was tempted to accept it. That is, until the head of the Department of Physiology at Ole Miss moved to North Dakota. What a stroke of luck! Suddenly, the perfect job in the perfect town at the perfect time was wide open to Ott. But like so many other things in Ott's life, this opportunity had a glitch.

Dr. David Pankratz, the new dean of the University of Mississippi Medical School, was not comfortable with the idea of allowing a physically handicapped man run one of his departments. Here is how Ott described the situation: "I applied for the position despite much foreboding by the dean of the medical school. Dr. David Pankratz did make me head of the department, but with much worry that I would not be able to stand up under the rigors of the job because of my polio. Fortunately, the head of the department usually has a number of other people who can work for him and can do the work that is required by muscles. We had quite a number of student assistants, and by that time, I had received some federal research grants that gave us a reasonable amount of money to hire technicians to work with me in research. It turns out that these were the first research grants from the federal government that had been received at the University of Mississippi."

And these grants would not be the last, as Ott's research ignited a surge of cash flow into the University of Mississippi, the likes of which had never been seen before. Dr. David Pankratz would have made a colossal blunder, indeed, had he not hired Ott. As it turns out, he was the best thing that had ever happened to Ole Miss.

Ott's career wasn't the only thing going well for him in 1948. On May 14th of the same year, a new baby blessed the Guyton household. John Richard was born only two years behind his brother Robert, who was two years younger than David. Ott was creating his own little Guyton Gang. He and Ruth couldn't have been happier. That is, until their fourth child was born just two years later. On June 20, 1950, the Guyton Gang expanded to include Steven William. And for the first time in Ott's adult life, he actually had some spare time to spend with his big beloved family.

Left to right: John, Steven with Ott, David, baby Catherine with Ruth, and Robert, 1951

After three years of happy sameness, things became even better for the Guytons, and for the state of Mississippi. Until then, Ruth and Ott had only little boy children, and Ole Miss had only a two-year medical program. All of that changed in 1951. With spring in the air, plans were finally put into action to build a long-awaited, four-year medical school in the state's capital city, Jackson. Until this point, the only medical program in the state had been Ole Miss's two-year program, of which Ott's father was the dean. (Just as a side note, the location of the new medical school was to be on the grounds of an old insane asylum).

The changes in the Guyton family began on July 18th with the birth of Catherine Anne, the couple's first baby girl. This wonderful change in the Guyton trend seemed to be a sign of things to come. Also that same year, the United States Junior Chamber of Commerce chose Ott as one of the ten most outstanding young men in America! Arthur C. Guyton was no longer only a local hero. He was now beginning to be recognized all over the country for his various achievements.

With plans for a four-year college in the works, the Guytons knew that it was only a matter of time before the gang would have to leave their beloved Oxford behind. Despite a slight mourning for Oxford, the Guytons were thrilled by the prospect of what a four-year medical school

Arthur and his father Billy talking to members of the U.S. Junior Chamber of Commerce at the awards banquet for the ten most outstanding young men in America. Dayton, Ohio, 1951

Six Guyton children (Cathy, Steve, John, Robert, David, and baby Jeannie) pose in an electric motorcar, which they built themselves under Ott's supervision. 1955

could mean to Mississippi (which was experiencing a shortage of doctors since the end of World War II). The construction of the new college had not even begun yet, but with the new baby girl, the recent award, and things going well for Ott both personally and professionally, optimism reigned in the Guyton household.

Three years after the birth of Ott's first daughter, baby Catherine's wish for a little sister was granted. Jean Margaret was born on December 9, 1954, the same year that the new medical school should have been completed. However, due to construction delays, the University

Hospital was not officially opened for business until July 1, 1955. "We hated very badly to leave the environment of the University in Oxford, and we hated to leave the community of Oxford itself," Ott admitted. But, the new university was a powder keg of opportunity for Ott's research, ideas, and teaching. The family soon settled into their new town, and began construction of the family home...a project entirely born and implemented of Ott's genius, and carried out by his own little "army" of Guytons.

Ott created the idea for and directed the construction of what became one of the first concrete homes in Mississippi. Ott logically chose concrete to make the house fireproof. Ott's wife Ruth recalled, "Arthur designed and constructed the family house on what later became Meadow Road using two concrete mixers, quantities of concrete, ordinary day labor, and 'family manpower.'"

Although the construction of "the big house" (as it came to be known) was conducted in his free time, Ott's mind was never idle at the construction site. He was constantly inventing new methods of construction to make the building more efficient, sturdy, safe, and practical. As his oldest son David later jested, some of Ott's construction inventions were more successful than others. "He was especially proud of his invention of reusable concrete pouring forms [which worked well (he thrived on methods for mass production)]. But the plan for maintaining a two-inch pool of water on the roof [so that evaporation would keep the house cool] never worked because of leaks under the poured

"The big house" in Jackson, Mississippi, was on a fifteen-acre plot of woodlands. The hallway to the bedrooms was so long that the children sometimes used it as a bowling alley. 1960

concrete rim around the edge of the roof, which dripped water over the edge of the roof for days after any rain!" I guess you can't win them all.

By 1958, "the big house" was finally complete, but the Guytons actually moved in a couple of years before it was entirely finished. Soon after the move, the Guytons welcomed another child into their home and lives. It was June 13, 1956, when Ruth presented Ott with their seventh child, Douglas Charles.

Just how many children were in the Guyton family? Well, the final Guyton-family count was a total of two adults and ten children living in a 1-story, 127-foot-long, 17-room home. James Lawrence was born December 30, 1959,

Thomas Scott was born November 14, 1961, and Gregory Paul was born May 31, 1967. Although Ott originally stated that he wanted to have twenty children, he never complained about receiving only half that number. The Guytons were often teased about their large number of children, which they always bore with good-humored dignity. But when asked in earnest why they had so many kids, Ruth replied, "The incredible truth is, simply, that we happen to like children."

Obviously the 50s and 60s were Ott's most productive family years; but, they were also his most productive years at University Medical Center (UMC). From a series of experiments Ott began during his first years in Jackson, he began to discover and prove that there were major flaws in some commonly believed theories on circulatory function.

Circulatory function is the way the blood flows through your body. It is very important that doctors fully understand it, because many of the most serious illnesses and causes of death in humans are due to some type of abnormality in this area. As it turns out, doctors didn't understand it as well as they thought they did. And some of the things they thought they knew turned out to be just plain wrong.

The major theoretical flaw that most doctors strongly believed at the time was that the heart was in control of how much blood it pumped, when it is actually the kidneys that determine this. This major scientific and medical breakthrough became clear in 1966 when Ott's department at the university obtained its first computer. Using his knowledge of electronics, and designing the world's largest mathemati-

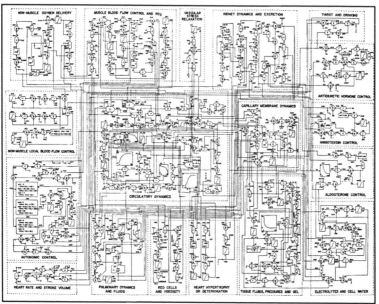

This is a diagram Ott made (greatly reduced in size) of the systems analysis he used to explain regulation of the circulatory system to students and colleagues.

cal model of the circulatory system (consisting of more than four hundred equations), Ott was able to prove the true relationship between blood, veins, heart, and kidneys, and that kidneys are the true regulators of long-term blood pressure control. This discovery, in a slightly more complex form, became known as the Theory of Infinite Gain. This theory is the major reason that many people around the world consider Arthur C. Guyton to be the Father of Modern Cardiovascular Physiology. Ott's research on this topic has led to many changes in the way doctors treat their patients, and as a result has saved countless lives. It has also contributed to a plethora of additional studies to further promote the understanding of circulatory function. Perhaps the most interesting thing about Ott's theory is that he attributed his findings, in large measure, to the lessons he learned as a child while building and fixing things, and through his work (or play) with electronics.

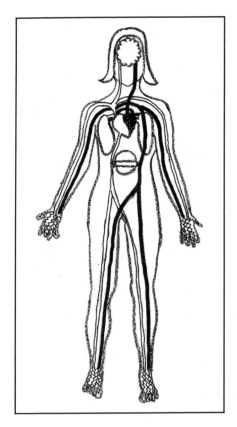

Blood flows through the vessels of your body to deposit oxygen and nutrients, and to take away waste products. There are three kinds of blood vessels: (1.) Arteries, the thick black lines of the diagram, carry blood loaded with oxygen from your heart to cells and organs.
(2.) Capillaries, the tiny zigzag lines, function the same as the arteries but are much smaller. (3.) Veins, the hollow white lines, have unloaded their oxygen, and are returning to the heart for reoxygenation.

Until Ott's famous discoveries, doctors and scientists thought that the heart determined blood flow, when it was actually the kidneys.

9

Guytonians

*If we, as his former students,
have achieved success in our fields,
it is because we have stood on the
shoulders of a giant.*

—John Hall (proud Guytonian)

For the next forty-two years, Ott changed the lives of people everywhere through his research and his teaching. He wrote or edited well over forty scientific books and six hundred scientific papers. But his most famous literary work, and his most powerful teaching tool, was his *Textbook of Medical Physiology.* This textbook, first published in 1956, immediately went down in history as one of the only med-

Guytonian, Joseph Bosarge, still frequently consults his copy of Textbook of Medical Physiology.

ical textbooks written by a sole author. Usually it takes several extremely intelligent people many years to combine so much detailed scientific information into an organized, useful manuscript. Ott did it alone, in one year, using the notes that he used in his teaching lectures. Although the most recent editions of the textbook were co-authored by one of Ott's former students, John Hall, Ott was still able to put ten children through college and medical school on the royalties that he received from the sale of his textbook. It remains the best-selling medical textbook of all time.

After a lifetime of fantastic accomplishments, while still going strong with his research and teaching, Ott was finally honored in a manner befitting his achievements. On August 25, 1989, Ott and Ruth dressed in their Sunday best, and headed through the busy streets of downtown Jackson to the Mississippi Trade Mart. There they met over one thousand of Ott's closest friends, family, colleagues, students, and admirers. It was a steamy Mississippi summer afternoon, and Ott was, perhaps for the first time in his life, unprepared. Indeed, nothing could have prepared him for the overwhelming sentiment felt on that special day.

The entire day had actually been planned many months before Ott and Ruth began their journey to the Trade Mart. It was on March 13, 1989, that a special joint session of the House Chamber (later echoed in the Senate) was called to order especially in honor of Ott. With the passage of Resolutions 564 and 638, all members of Congress agreed to create an official day to recognize Ott's contributions to science, medicine, society, our country, and humanity. As a result, August 25, 1989, was to be officially declared "Arthur C. Guyton Day," and was to be celebrated appropriately. Indeed it was. The celebration actually lasted for two days, culminating in a humble, grateful, and emotional acceptance speech by Ott himself.

Among those who attended the celebration were many of the lucky scholars that Ott taught, who now proudly call themselves "Guytonians." Of this fortunate group, nearly

Ott addresses the legislature at a special joint session in the House Chamber that was held in his honor.

thirty now chair their own departments at various universities, and six were American Physiological Society presidents. Perhaps this is because Ott set a new standard for teaching at UMC and around the world. He always found time to help his students, or simply to discuss their ideas, no matter how busy he was. But more importantly, Ott never "poked information into his students," like many of his predecessors. Instead, he offered them a strong foundation of concepts to base their own ideas upon. He did not teach them…he simply helped them to learn on their own. He actually made learning a pleasant experience. According to most Guytonians, Ott's teaching style was all his own.

One particular Guytonian, Dr. Atkinson W. Longmire of Silver Spring, Maryland, described a typical example of Ott's unique teaching methods. "The year was 1963, my first year of medical school. I was in Dr. Guyton's class preparing to take the very first medical school exam of my life. Everyone was horribly nervous, and no one knew what to expect. I looked down at the first question on the page, and read the words 'Why does the heart pump blood?'" Dr. Longmire was certainly no expert on heart function at that point in his educational career, but he did know enough to realize that there was no way to correctly answer that question within the confines of this exam, if he could answer it at all. "I actually don't even remember my own answer to the question, but I do remember one of the other student's responses, as it was such a funny and ridiculous answer. His name was Thurston, I believe, and he wrote 'because the

Ott lectures future Guytonians at the University of Mississippi School of Medicine. 1989

sodium pump has enough to do.' After the exam, and comparing answers, the students complained about the question to Dr. Guyton. His response was surprising. He simply smiled and said, 'There is no right or wrong answer to that question. I just wanted to know how you think.'" Dr. Longmire, like so many other Guytonians, went on to pursue a distinguished career in research and medicine, and is now a medical officer for OSHA (the U.S. Department of Labor's Occupational Safety and Health Administration) Office of Occupational Medicine.

10

The Death of
a Legend

*I hope to live a life that is considerably
less stressful and strenuous
than the life that I have lived thus far.*
—Arthur C. Guyton

Two weeks following "Arthur C. Guyton Day," on his
70th birthday, Ott officially retired as the chairman of the
Department of Physiology and Biophysics at the University
of Mississippi Medical Center; yet that did not put an end to
Ott's career. He continued teaching at the university and
editing his textbooks until he was eighty-three years old.

Here is how another Guytonian, Dr. Joseph R. Bosarge of Jacksonville, Florida, described Ott's second-to-last lecture at the University of Mississippi Medical Center:

I remember showing up for class that day, and everyone being really excited about Dr. Guyton's lecture. At that point, we all knew that he would be retiring from teaching soon, and that it would be one of his last lectures. Most students even brought their copies of Textbook of Medical Physiology *for him to sign. It was apparent to everyone that we were witnessing something historically important.*

Ott explains his computer model of the cardiovascular system to medical students in 1989.

When Dr. Guyton arrived, a very noisy class of one hundred people quieted down very quickly. Although he was very soft spoken, Dr. Guyton always managed to hold everyone's attention quite effortlessly. Unlike most professors, who often begin their lectures behind a podium flipping through slides on a film projector or computer presentation, Dr. Guyton simply greeted students from his wheelchair in front of the auditorium, then randomly selected one unsuspecting student from the audience (me) to assist him with the first part of the lecture.

Dr. Guyton handed me a regular-size sheet of notebook paper, and asked me to hold it up high so that the entire class could see it. As I displayed this rather unimpressive item, trying hard to conceal my confusion at the strange request, Dr. Guyton announced in his soft voice that 'This was what we knew about the circulatory system and blood pressure control when I first got started in this business.' As I stood there holding the tiny sheet of paper, Dr. Guyton gave an overview of the journey through various scientific discoveries leading to the truth about this complex web of bodily function.

Then Dr. Guyton asked me to hold up another piece of paper. But unlike the first one, this paper was huge, at least four feet by four feet square, that still had his meticulously neat handwriting on it, with lines carefully weaving all of the different processes of circulatory function and blood pressure regulation together into an enormously complex diagram. Then he simply stated that 'This is what we know now about the circulatory system and blood pressure control.' We were all especially impressed, not just with the intricate diagram, or the scientific advancement, but with the man standing before us, who made the advancement possible.

Like so many Guytonians before him, Dr. Bosarge went on to make headlines in the areas of research and medicine. In May 2004, he became the first student to graduate from the University of Mississippi Medical Center earning both M.D. and Ph.D. degrees simultaneously. Unfortunately, Dr. Guyton did not survive to witness this historic occasion.

On April 3, 2003, Ott and his wife were in a car accident not far from the "the big house" in Jackson, Mississippi. Ott was pronounced dead that day at the University of Mississippi Medical Center, the same institu-

Ott was laid to rest in St. Peter's Cemetery in Oxford, Mississippi, after a tearful funeral at Oxford University Methodist Church. He was joined in rest by Ruth just a few days later.

tion that he proudly served for so many years. His wife, Ruth, died seven days later from her injuries. The following year, Ott's oldest son David related some of his father's last wishes to graduating medical students during a commencement address at UMC. David assured the graduating class that there was no place on earth his father would rather have been during his last moments than the University of Mississippi Medical Center. He got his wish. Ott died surrounded by merely a few of the millions of scholars that he helped to train. And his legacy lives on.

The Guyton Legacy

Ruth was the greatest thing that ever happened to me in my life. It was her willingness to have ten children that made our family what it is.

—Arthur C. Guyton

According to Ott, his greatest accomplishment was his family. Ott and Ruth Guyton were survived by ten children, all Harvard-educated physicians, who today live all over the country helping others in need.

This photograph shows Ott and Ruth with their entire Guyton family. 1989

The children of Ruth and Arthur Guyton

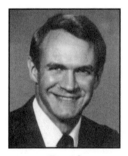

David
Baltimore, Maryland

Robert
Atlanta, Georgia

John
Durham, North
Carolina

Steven
Seattle, Washington

Catherine Greenberger
Sewickley, Pennsylvania

Jean Gispen
Oxford, Mississippi

Douglas
Reno, Nevada

James
Memphis, Tennessee

Thomas
Memphis, Tennessee

Gregory
Baltimore, Maryland

Due to his family alone, Ott reserved a special place in pop culture history by inspiring features in *People Magazine, Reader's Digest, 20/20,* and the *Oprah Winfrey Show.* He was also survived by thirty-two grandchildren, two great-grandchildren, his sister Ruth, and his brother William.

Ott's first textbook, *Textbook of Medical Physiology,* is now in it's tenth edition, and has been published in fifteen different languages. It is the best-selling physiology textbook in the world, and the best-selling medical textbook of all time. The concepts in this textbook will continue to help train physicians all over the world for years to come.

Ott's innovative research has inspired an infinite number of new research ideas that build upon his groundbreaking discoveries about circulatory function. They have become the base-point for a multitude of new discoveries and possibilities having to do with blood flow, heart function, kidney function, and more. The computer model that Ott used to illustrate his theories on circulatory function has even been adapted for use by NASA to help scientists discover how long-term weightlessness affects the body.

At least three of Ott's medical inventions: the locking and unlocking (walking) leg brace, the handicapped hoist, and the modern electric wheelchair, are still widely used devices in healthcare today.

Arthur C. Guyton's contributions to science have generated more than four million dollars from the National Institutes of Health (NIH) for the Department of Physiology

This is one of four hoists in Ott's home in Jackson, Mississippi. He used this one to get in and out of bed. 1999

ABOVE: Two young polio survivors exercise their limbs using the walking leg braces that Ott invented. 1950

RIGHT: Ott spends some quality time with his son David, who enjoys riding in Ott's latest invention, the modern electric wheelchair. 1947

at UMC since 1968, and that number is still rising as the grant is renewed every five years. This grant, established based on the foundations of Dr. Guyton's research, is one of the longest-running grants in the history of the NIH. Among other things, this fact catapulted Ott to legendary status at the NIH and at UMC.

Fellow polio sufferer, President Franklin D. Roosevelt, dedicated the new NIH campus in Bethesda on October 31, 1940, just eight years before Ott's grant began. This event was held to celebrate NIH's historic move from one building in Washington, D.C., to its new campus setting in Maryland on forty-five acres of land donated by Luke and Helen Wilson.

Ott received an astonishing number of awards and honors for his contributions to science and medicine. Among these are every conceivable physiology honor you can think of. These are listed in the "Selected Accomplishments" section at the back of this book. Ott claimed one of these honors as dearest to his heart, thus I will mention it here. It was the honor of being asked to give the William Harvey Lecture for the Royal College of Physicians in London at the 400th anniversary of the birth of William Harvey in 1978. William Harvey was the world-famous scientist and fellow innovative mind who first described the circulation of the blood through the body. He was Ott's greatest predecessor in the study of human physiology.

This is the same building (the "Shannon Building") today. It now serves as NIH headquarters in the heart of the campus in Bethesda, Maryland.

From keeping up with the family's hats to keeping up with an entire generation of medical students' educations, Ott's life has been a roller coaster of learning experiences. It was clear from a very young age that he would not be limited or intimidated by the idea of any difficult project, conquest, or intellectual pursuit. Instead Ott used logic and the lessons of his youth throughout his life to isolate any problem, then to simply find a solution. He did not seem to recognize the word impossible. As a result, he excelled at nearly every challenge he faced…even paralysis. Over time, Ott became nationally, and even internationally, known for various contributions in the areas of science, medicine, modern technology, patriotism, and humanity. But to Ott, the most precious of his accomplishments was his family. Indeed, his entire life, as stated in the dedication of each of his medical textbooks, was devoted to the people he loved the most:

Dedicated to

MY FATHER
For the uncompromising principles that guided his life

MY MOTHER
For leading her children into intellectual pursuits

MY WIFE
For her magnificent devotion to her family

MY CHILDREN
For making everything worthwhile

Arthur C. Guyton
Photo Album

Oxford Square in the 1920s. This is what Ott's hometown looked like when he grew up.

It is easy to see from this photograph why Ott loved her so much. This photograph shows the kind and loving smile of Ruth Weigle Guyton, the woman whom Ott often credited as the source of all things good in his life.

Several years after Ott was infected with polio, there was a terrible epidemic of the disease in America. This photo shows a member of the Polio Eradication Campaign radioing informa-tion to headquarters during the epidemic of 1963.

Huge quantities of polio vaccine were produced and shipped all over the country from Alabama. Here the Alabama National Guard prepares to fly polio vaccine from Birmingham to Haleyville during the epidemic of 1963.

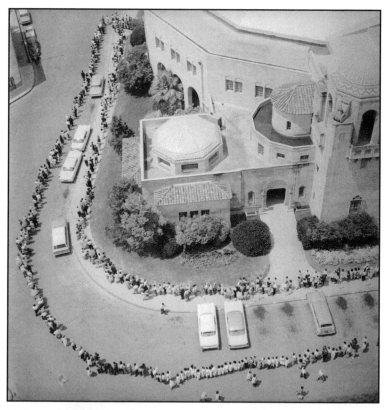

Folks stood in line for hours all over the country to receive the vaccine. This photograph shows an aerial view of a crowd surrounding a massive city auditorium in San Antonio, Texas, awaiting the polio immunization. Unfortunately, the vaccine was produced too late to help Ott.

The four children of Kate and Billy Guyton are all grown up in this 1971 photograph taken at Dr. Billy Guyton's funeral. They are from left to right: Ruth, Ott, Bill, and Jack.

Despite Ott's challenges in life, the Guyton home was always a happy one. There was never a dull moment at the family dinner table. 1969

All of Ott's children enjoyed athletics. Here eight of Ott and Ruth's ten children enjoy a friendly game of football in their front yard.

The living room of "the big house" was a special place for sharing and caring for the Guyton family. Here they played games, discussed important family events, and simply enjoyed each other's company.

One of the qualities that made Ott so unique was his ability to connect with others. His students and colleagues alike considered him more than simply a mentor...he was also a friend. He always had time to care about the concerns of others.

Those who knew Ott best from his years at UMC remember him just as he is in this photograph: at his desk, buried in his work, but with a welcome smile on his face to greet anyone who happens to drop by for a visit. His door was always open, especially for his students.

Just weeks before Ott's retirement as chairman of the Department of Physiology at UMC, he was honored by an extremely official celebration. This photograph shows Ott addressing well-wishers at the Mississippi Trade Mart on August 25, 1989, Arthur C. Guyton Day.

It was only after more than fifty years of independent living, that the deterioration of old age forced Ott to reuse some of the methods of getting around that he learned in Warm Springs, Georgia, after first contracting polio. This photograph shows a ramp that Ott was able to transfer onto, from his wheelchair, and then inch his way down and into the Guyton's homemade swimming pool at "the big house."

This is how Ott looked shortly before he died. It was not until he was eighty years old that he came to truly depend upon his own medical inventions. Although he did not like the confinement of his wheelchair, Ott bore the burden of old age as gracefully as anyone could. Until the very end, he was a man of great strength and character.

Ott and Ruth may be gone now, but they will never be forgotten. This is a picture of Ott's oldest son, David, lecturing medical students at the University of Mississippi Medical Center. The picture on the screen is of Ruth Guyton, his mother.

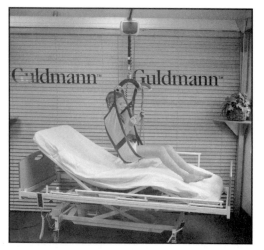

Here is a modern day spin-off of the human hoist that Ott invented. There are now many variations of this product that has helped millions of disabled individuals gain independence.

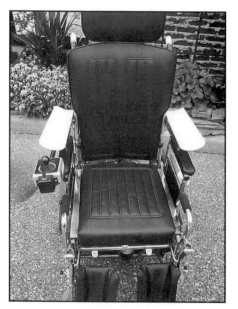

This is a modern version of the electric wheelchair that Ott invented, then sold to a company called Everest and Jennings for merely $100.00. When asked why he gained so little for his invention, he often replied, "I didn't want to make money from people with polio."

Since the days Ott roamed the campus of Fort Detrick, Maryland, it has become a research hub of the National Cancer Institute. Here is what the main gate looks like today.

This photograph was taken at the Guyton family reunion at Ole Miss in front of Guyton Hall in July 2004.

Selected List of Accomplishments

Societies and Organizations

AOA, Harvard (Honorary Scholastic Society)

SIGMA XI, Harvard (Honorary Scientific Society)

ODK (Honorary Leadership Society)

OKU, University of Mississippi Dental School (Honorary Dental Society)

American Physiological Society (President-elect, 1973–74; President, 1974-75)

Editor-in-Chief, International Review of Physiology (1973–1983)

Editor, Cardiovascular Volume of International Review of Physiology (1973–1983)

Federation of American Societies of Experimental Biology (Council 1974–77; President 1975–76)

Biophysical Society

Southern Society for Clinical Research (Secretary-Treasurer, 1953–56, President 1956–57)

Executive Committee Oak Ridge Institute of Nuclear Studies Teletherapy Evaluation Board (1952–53)

Neurophysiological Group of American Physiological Society

Mississippi Heart Association (Vice President, 1952–54; President-Elect, 1954–55; President, 1955–56)

American Heart Association (Policy Committee, 1960–61; Board of Directors, 1961–67; Publications Board, 1971–77)

Advisory Council of Circulation Section of the American Heart Association

Advisory Board of Council for High Blood Pressure Research

Mississippi Academy of Science (Board of Directors, 1961–67; President, 1967–68)

International Society for Hypertension

Biomedical Engineering Society

Member of the Harvard Medical School Alumni Council (1989–1991)

Foreign Member, Russian Academy of Natural Sciences (1992)

Honorary Foreign Member, Argentine College of Venous and Lymphatic Surgery (1992)

Honors and Awards

Amateur Radio License (1936–1979)

Commercial Radio License (1937–1940)

Selected as One of the Ten Most Outstanding Young Men of America by the United States Junior Chamber of Commerce (1951)

United States Presidential Citation for Development of Aid for Handicapped Person (1956)

Ida B. Gould Award for Cardiovascular Research (American Association for the Advancement of Science – 1959)

Silver Medallion Award for Research (Mississippi Heart Association – 1961)

First Federal of Mississippi Award for Contributions to the State of Mississippi (1966)

E. A. Rovenstine Memorial Award Lecturer of the American Society of Anesthesiologists (1967)

Wiggers Award of the Circulation Group of the American Physiological Society for Cardiovascular Research (1972)

Honors and Awards *(continued)*

ALZA Award and Lecturer for Biomedical Engineering Research (1972)

A. Ross McIntyre Award for Contributions to Medical Teaching and Research (University of Nebraska – 1972)

Leonard and Lillian Ratner Award and Lectureship (1973)

Distinguished Physiology Lectureship Award (1973)

American Heart Association Annual Research Achievement Award (1974)

American Heart Association Annual Research Achievement Award (1975)

Dickinson Richards Award of the Pulmonary Council of the American Heart Association for Cardiopulmonary Research (1975)

Honorary Fellow of American College of Cardiology (1975)

The Annual Physiology Teaching Award of the Association of Charimen of Departments of Physiology (1975)

University of Mississippi Hall of Fame (1975)

Annual Ravdin Lecturer of the American Surgical Society (1975)

Outstanding Contributions Award of the Mississippi Academy of Science (1976)

Distinguished Alumnus Award of Phi Kappa Phi National Scholarship Honor Society (1976)

Theobald Smith Lectureship Award (Albany Medical College – 1977)

Baxter Travenol Lectureship Award of the International Anesthesia Research Society (1977)

Doctor of Science Honorary Degree, Medical College of Wisconsin (1977)

Walter E. MacPherson Lectureship Award (1977)

The Harvey Lecture, 400th Anniversary Symposium on the Occasion of the Birth of William Harvey, Discoverer of the Circulation, Royal College of Physicians London, England (1978)

First Annual Evan Jones Memorial Lecture, University of London, St. Thomas' Hospital (1979)

Founder's Award, Southern Society of Clinical Investigation (1979)

Einthoven Lecture, (Leiden, Holland – 1979)

Einthoven Medal, Holland (1979)

George Griffith Memorial Lectureship Award (California Heart Association – 1980)

James A. Stevenson Memorial Lecturer (Canada – 1980)

Fiftieth Anniversary of the Mississippi Academy of Science Award for Outstanding Contributions to the Academy (1980)

Fiftieth Anniversary of the Mississippi Academy of Science Award for Outstanding Contributions in Mississippi (1980)

Fiftieth Anniversary of the Mississippi Academy of Science Award for Outstanding Contributions to the Advancement of Science (1980)

CIBA Award for Research in Hypertension (1980)

James Shephenson Lectureship Award of the University of London (1980)

Annual Daggs Award for Contributions to Physiology and to the Society (1981)

Mellon Award of the University of Pittsburg (1981)

Amateaur Radio Extra-Class License (1981–2003)

Jenssen Award Lecture of the Society of Cardiovascular Anesthesiologists (1982)

Honorary Doctor of Medicine Degree (Pretoria, South Africa – 1982)

Alvin F. Rieck Memorial Lecture (1982)

Honors and Awards *(continued)*

Third International Society for the Study of Hypertension in Pregnancy (Keynote Speaker – 1982)

Mississippian of the Year (1983)

E.S. Meyers Memorial Lecture (Brisbane, Australia – 1983)

Annual Student Lecture, University of Iowa School of Medicine (1983)

Pfizer Visiting Professor to the Medical Schools of Australia (1983)

Biannual Merk, Sharp and Dohme International Award for Research in Hypertension (Interlaken, Switzerland – 1984)

Annual Invited Professor Lectureship for the Department of Physiology (University of Texas – 1984)

Mississippian of the Year (1984)

Schumacher Lecture in Anesthesiology (Baylor School of Medicine – 1984)

Advisory Committee to the Director of the National Institutes of Health (1985–1987)

Inaugural "Donald Chapman Visiting Professor Lecture" (Baylor School of Medicine – 1985)

One of Five "Mississippians Who Have Achieved Success: Mississippi Style" by the Mississippi Chapter of the American Cancer Society

One of Three "Fathers Day" Fathers for the Jackson, Mississippi, area (VIP Magazine – 1985)

Honoree at a Symposium Entitled "The Guyton Years–Physiology in Mississippi" (Organized and Arranged by Former and Present Students, Fellows, and Colleagues – 1985)

Welcome Visiting Professor to Texas College of Osteopathic Medicine (1986)

Macallum Lectureship (University of Toronto – 1986)

"The Highest Effort" Award in Science (National Sigma Epsilon Fraternity – 1986)

"Faculty Member to Be Saluted" (American Association of Higher Education and Carnegie Foundation for the Advancement of Teaching – 1987)

Commendations from the Mississippi House of Representatives and the Mississippi Senate for Teaching (1987)

William Harvey Award of the American Society of Hypertension (1988)

Honorary Doctor of Medicine Degree (Murcia, Spain – 1989)

Special Scientific Achievement Award of the American Medical Association (1990)

Mikamo Award (Makuhari, Japan – 1992)

Elected to Russian Academy of Natural Sciences (1992)

American College of Physicians Award for Outstanding Work in Science Related to Medicine (1992)

Keynote Speaker, 21st Annual John C. Forbes Honors Colloquium, Medical College of Virginia (1993)

First Distinguished Investigator Award of the Consortium of Southeastern Hypertension Centers (1995)

Abraham Flexner Award for Distinguished Service to Medical Education, Association of American Medical Colleges (1996)

Distinguished Service Award, Association of Chairs of Departments of Physiology (1996)

Eugene Braunwald Award for Mentorship (American Heart Assocaition – 2001)

Selected Publications

These are Ott's publications that he felt were the most significant of his career.

Guyton, A. C., Hall, John E. *Pocket Companion to Textbook of Medical Physiology,* W. B. Saunders Company ©1998, 2001

Guyton, A. C., *Textbook of Medical Physiology, 10th Edition,* W. B. Saunders Company ©2000

Guyton, A. C., *Function of the Human Body, 6th Edition,* W. B. Saunders Company ©1984

Guyton, A. C., *Human Physiology and Mechanisms of Disease,* Six Editions, W. B. Saunders Company ©1987–1996

Guyton, A. C., *Basic Human Physiology: Normal Function and Mechanisms of Disease,* Two Editions, W. B. Saunders Company ©1971, 1977

Guyton, A. C., *Basic Neuroscience: Anatomy and Physiology,* Two Editions, W. B. Saunders Company ©1987, 1991

Guyton, A. C., Jones, C. E., Coleman, T. G., *Circulatory Physiology: Cardiac Output and Its Regulation, 2nd Edition,* W. B. Saunders Company ©1975

Guyton, A. C., Taylor, A. E., and Granger, H. J., *Circulatory Physiology II: Dynamics and Control of the Body Fluid,* W. B. Saunders Company ©1975

Guyton, A. C., *Circulatory Physiology III: Arterial Pressure and Hypertension,* W. B. Saunders Company ©1980

Guyton, A. C. and Jones, C. E. (eds.), *International Review of Physiology: Circulation, Volume I,* Butterworth ©1974

Guyton, A. C. and Cowley, A. W., Jr. (eds.), *International Review of Physiology: Circulation, Volume II,* University Park Press ©1976

Guyton, A. C. and Young, D. B. (eds.), *International Review of Physiology: Circulation, Volume III,* University Park Press ©1979

Guyton, A. C., "Determination of Cardiac Output by Equating Venous Return Curves With Cardiac Response Curves," *Physiological Reviews 35:12* ©1955

Guyton, A. C., "Peripheral Circulation," *Annual Review of Physiology 21:239* ©1959

Guyton, A. C., "A concept of negative interstitial pressure based on pressures in implanted perforated capsules," *Circulation Research 12:399–414* ©1963

Guyton, A. C. "Venous Return," *Handbook of Physiology 32:1099–1133* ©1963

Guyton, A. C., Langston, J. B., and Navar, G., "Theory for renal autoregulation by feedback at the juxtaglomerular apparatus," *Circulation Research 14:(1) 187–197* ©1964

Guyton, A. C. and Coleman, T. G., "Long-term regulation of the circulation: Interrelationships with body fluid volumes," *Physical Bases of Circulatory Transport Regulation and Exchange,* W. B. Saunders Company ©1967

Guyton, A. C., Taylor, A. E., Granger, H. J., and Coleman, T. G., "Interstitial fluid pressure," *Physiology Review 51:527–563* ©1971

Guyton, A. C., Coleman, T. G., and Granger, H. J., "Circulation: Overall Regulation," *Annual Review of Physiology 34:13–46* ©1972

Guyton, A. C., Coleman, T. G., Cowley, A. W., Jr., Scheel, K. W., Manning, R. D., Jr., and Norman, R. A., Jr., "Arterial pressure regulation: Overriding dominance of the kidneys in long-term regulation and in hypertension," *Hypertension Manual 111–134,* New York Medical Books ©1973

Guyton, A. C., Lindsey, A. W., "Effect of elevated blood protein concentration on the development of pulmonary edema," *Circulation Research 7:649–657* ©1959 *Current Contents 29:15* ©1986

Acknowledgments and Picture Credits

I am extremely grateful to the Guyton children and to the University of Mississippi Medical Center for sharing their memories and photographs not specifically credited below, especially to John Guyton and Jay Ferchaud, who helped me with this project far above and beyond the call of duty. I would also like to gratefully acknowledge Dalton Patterson for helping me to see things from a kid's point of view. Thank you.

Annual Review of Physiology: 75

Bosarge, Jerusha: 10, 24, 29, 76, 78

Fizer, Mike via the Aircraft Owners and Pilots Association (AOPA): 28

Guldmann, Inc.: 104 (top)

Jordan, Robert and the University of Mississippi Imaging Services: 85

Lader, Beverly and Marvin: 104 (bottom)

Longmire, Sarah and Aerial: 52, 105 (top)

National Institute of Health Almanac – Historical Photos: 92, 93

National Lipid Association: 44 (left), 53

Public Health Image Library (CDC/Charles Farmer): Leg Brace – 91

Public Health Image Library (CDC): 61 (right)

Public Health Image Library (CDC Dr. Joseph J. Esposito): 61 (middle)

Public Health Image Library (CDC S. Smith): 97, 98

Sgro, Jean Yves: 61 (left)

Towe Ford Museum, Deer Lodge, Montana: 13

United States Army Garrison (USAG) Fort Detrick, Maryland: 54, 55, 56

Bibliography

The Arthur C. Guyton Archives. "The Guyton Biography." Jackson, Mississippi: The University of Mississippi Medical Center. 2004. http://www.umc.edu/guyton/bio.html.

The Arthur C. Guyton Archives. "The Guyton Children." Jackson, Mississippi: The University of Mississippi Medical Center. 2004. http://www.umc.edu/guyton/children.html.

The Arthur C. Guyton Archives. "The Guyton Obituary." Jackson, Mississippi: The University of Mississippi Medical Center. 2004. http://www.umc.edu/guyton/TheGuytonObituary.html.

The Arthur C. Guyton Archives. "Honors and Awards." Jackson, Mississippi: The University of Mississippi Medical Center. 2004. http://www.umc.edu/guyton/honors.html.

The Arthur C. Guyton Archives. "A Legacy of Achievement." Jackson, Mississippi: The University of Mississippi Medical Center. 2004. http://www.umc.edu/guyton/index.html.

Author interview with Dr. A. W. (Jack) Longmire. March 16, 2005.

Author interview with Dr. David Guyton. January 15, 2005.

Author interview with Dr. John Guyton. January 30, 2004.

Author interview with Dr. Joseph Bosarge. March 15, 2005.

Bode R. "A doctor who's dad to seven doctors—so far!" *Reader's Digest*. December 1982:141–145.

Brinson, Carroll. *Arthur C. Guyton: His Life, His Family, His Achievements*. Jackson, Mississippi: Oakdale Press, 1989.

Calandra, Bob. "Arthur C. Guyton Dies." *The Scientist*. April 2003: http://www.biomedcentral.com/news/20030410/01/.

Guyton A. C., Lindsay A. W., and Kaufman B. N. "Effect of mean circulatory filling pressure and other Peripheral circulatory factors on cardiac output." *American Journal of Physiology 180:463–468*. 1955. http://ajplegacy.physiology.org/cgi/reprint/180/3/463.

Guyton, Arthur C., Coleman, T. G., Granger, H. J. "Circulation: Overall Regulation." *Annual Review of Physiology. Volume 34,* Pages 13–44. March 1972.

Guyton, Arthur C. *Textbook of Medical Physiology.* Philadelphia, Penn: W. B. Saunders Company. 1956.

Hall, John E. "The Pioneering Use of Systems Analysis to Study Cardiac Output Regulation" *American Journal of Physiology: Regulation Integration and Comparative Physiology 287:R1009–R1011.* 2004.

Henderson, Tom. *Image Formation and Detection, Lesson 6: The Eye.* The Physics Classroom. 1996–2004.

Houston, Laura. "Doctor Killed in Car Crash." *The Daily Mississippian.* University, Mississippi. April 07, 2003.

Keller, Candace E. "In Tribute: Past Rovenstine Lecturer Arthur C. Guyton, M.D. 1919–2003." American Society of Anesthesiologists. "ASA Newsletter." Administrative Update: Volume 67. July 2003.

The Oprah Winfrey Show. "Extraordinary Families: Medical Miracle" 2000. Official Transcript. http://www.oprah.com/tows/pastshows/tows_2000/tows_past_20001005_d.jhtml.

Owen, Brenda. "Arthur C. Guyton Day–Renowned Teacher, Researcher To Be Honored." U.S. House of Representatives. May 11, 1989. http://thomas.loc.gov/cgi-bin/query/z?r101:H11MY9-653.

The Oxford American Dictionary, Reissue Edition. Avon Publishing. 1982.

Quinn, Janis. "Medical Center Loses Celebrated Teacher, Legendary Writer, and Internationally Known Research Giants." *UMC News.* April 14, 2003.

Senate Concurrent Resolution No. 507. Mississippi Legislature, Regular Session 2004. Available online at http://billstatus.ls.state.ms.us/documents/2004/pdf/SC/SC0507SG.pdf.

Vatner, Stephen F. "In Memoriam: Arthur C. Guyton, M.D. (1919–2003)." *Circulation Research 2003:92:1272.* American Heart Association. http://circres.ahajournals.org/cgi/content/full/92/12/1272.

Index

G

H

I

J

L

M